Wonders Built by Humans

THE PYRAMIDS OF GIZA

Sloane Gould

CREATED BY Humans

Published in 2026 by The Rosen Publishing Group, Inc.
2544 Clinton Street, Buffalo, NY 14224

Editor: Kristen Nelson
Designer: Rachel Rising

Photo Credits: Cover, Guenter Albers/Shutterstock.com; Cover, (series background) Yuliya Chsherbakova/Shutterstock.com; p. 4 muratart/Shutterstock.com; p. 5 EaglePOV/Shutterstock.com; p. 7 Ikohan/Shutterstock.com; p. 9 Romain Biard/Shutterstock.com; p. 10 hemro/Shutterstock.com; p. 11 ErenMotion/Shutterstock.com; p. 13 Saint Images/Shutterstock.com; p. 14 Waj/Shutterstock.com; p. 15 AlexAnton/Shutterstock.com; p. 17 muratart/Shutterstock.com; p. 18 Colinmthompson/Shutterstock.com; p. 19 EaglePOV/Shutterstock.com; p. 21 AlexAnton/Shutterstock.com; p. 23 https://commons.wikimedia.org/wiki/File:Egypt._The_fourth_pyramid._Dr._Selim_Bey_Hassan%27s_excavations_close_to_4th_pyramid_in_progress_LOC_matpc.17973.jpg; p. 23 Aleksandra Tokarz/Shutterstock.com; p. 25 muratart/Shutterstock.com; p. 26 Waj/Shutterstock.com; p. 27 muratart/Shutterstock.com; p. 29 FRESHTIO IMAGERYgw28/Shutterstock.com.

Cataloging-in-Publication Data

Names: Gould, Sloane.
Title: The Pyramids of Giza / Sloane Gould.
Description: Buffalo, NY : Created by Humans, an imprint of Rosen Publishing, 2026. | Series: Wonders built by humans | Includes glossary and index.
Identifiers: ISBN 9781534553057 (pbk.) | ISBN 9781534553064 (library bound) | ISBN 9781534553071 (ebook)
Subjects: LCSH: Pyramids--Egypt--Jīzah--Juvenile literature. | Great Pyramid (Egypt)--Juvenile literature.
Classification: LCC DT63.G685 2026 | DDC 932.012--dc23

Manufactured in China

CPSIA Compliance Information: Batch #QWCBH26. For Further Information contact Rosen Publishing at 1-800-237-9932.

CONTENTS

AN ANCIENT WONDER

Earth is home to breathtaking landscapes and views. Tall mountains and deep oceans are natural wonders. But there are many wonders made by humans, too.

Ancient Greek travelers came up with a list of the seven wonders of the world about 2,500 years ago. Of those wonders of the ancient world, only one stands today—the Great Pyramid of Giza. This pyramid stands tall on the Giza **plateau** in Egypt with two other major pyramids beside it. Their massive sizes and genius designs inspired wonder in ancient people. Today, people come from around the world to see the pyramids!

How do you think the Great Pyramid has stayed standing while the other ancient wonders have turned to ruins?

WOW!

The original "Seven Wonders of the Ancient World" list included the Great Pyramid of Giza, the Hanging Gardens of Babylon, the Statue of Zeus (in Greece), and the Lighthouse of Alexandria.

ANCIENT EGYPT

Ancient Egyptians were the masterminds behind the Pyramids of Giza. The ancient Egyptian **civilization** started more than 5,000 years ago on the land around the Nile River. This is when the two kingdoms of Upper Egypt and Lower Egypt were united under one king. This king was the first pharaoh in a long line of pharaohs.

Ancient Egyptians invented a system of writing using pictures called hieroglyphics. That helped them record things that happened. They believed in many gods. They treated their pharaohs as gods on Earth. We know a lot about ancient Egypt because of the things that were left behind, including hieroglyphics, **artifacts**, and pyramids.

WOW!

Ancient Egyptians believed in more than 2,000 gods and goddesses, including Ra (god of the sun) and Osiris (god of the afterlife).

The ancient Egyptian civilization lasted more than 3,000 years!

WHAT ARE PYRAMIDS?

The ancient Egyptians left behind many stunning structures, from temples to palaces. However, they are most famous for their pyramids. All pyramids have a square base and four triangular sides. The sides meet at a point.

The first Egyptian pyramid was built around 2780 BCE for King Djoser (JOH-suhr). It was a step pyramid, or a pyramid with sides that rise up in steps. Later, Egyptians created smooth-sided pyramids. Some pyramids had **ornate** burial chambers, with all the riches that royalty would need in the afterlife. Some of the most famous pyramids are those in Giza because of their huge size.

WOW!

BCE means "Before Common Era" and CE means "Common Era," which started about 2,026 years ago.

Why are pyramids shaped like this? Egyptians may have believed it would help the pharaohs reach the heavens.

Djoser's Pyramid

Resting Places

Pyramids are where some of the most important people in Egyptian history are buried. Before pyramids, early Egyptian kings were laid to rest in *mastabas*. These mounds had a rectangular base, sloping sides, and a flat roof. They had different rooms, such as chapels and a burial chamber. After Djoser's pyramid was built, this new shape became the norm for pharaohs. Sometimes smaller pyramids or mastabas were found near the pharaoh's pyramid, which held their family and friends.

FOR THE PHARAOHS

In ancient Egypt, there was no one more important than the pharaoh. They led the people as the head of state, but also as religious leaders. Pharaohs oversaw war, taxes, and laws. They took part in ceremonies for the gods and goddesses. While there were some female pharaohs, including Cleopatra, most were male. The title of pharaoh went to the **heir** of the last pharaoh.

The Pyramids of Giza were made for pharaohs. Building these massive structures was back-breaking work. But the ancient Egyptians would do anything for their all-powerful leader.

King Khufu

The three pyramids of Giza were made for three pharaohs: Khufu (KOO-foo), his son Khafre (KAHF-ray), and Khafre's son Menkaure (mehn-KOW-ray).

KHUFU'S PYRAMID

The largest pyramid of Giza is called the Great Pyramid, or the Pyramid of Khufu. It was the tallest building in the world for around 3,800 years. The huge structure was about 482 feet (147 m) tall when it was first built. It's about 30 feet (10 m) shorter today because of **erosion**.

The Great Pyramid was covered in white limestone. It likely looked like it was shining in the bright desert sun. Inside, the pyramid was mostly solid stone. However, there were several passageways, shafts, and chambers. Khufu's body was put in a **sarcophagus** in a chamber in the center of the pyramid once he died.

WOW!

The Great Pyramid was built 4,500 years ago!

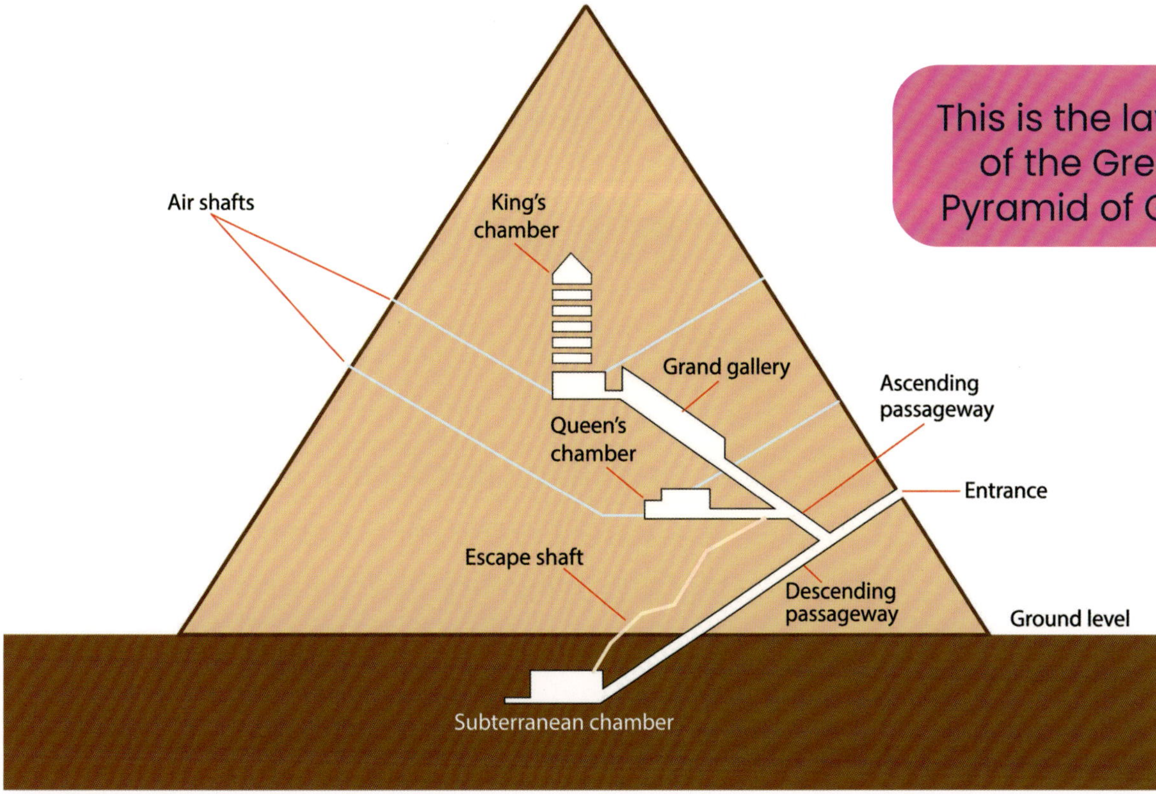

This is the layout of the Great Pyramid of Giza.

Ready for the Afterlife

Though very little is known about Khufu, his name lives on in the pyramid he ordered to be built. The pyramid complex of Giza tells us about what Khufu believed he might need for the afterlife. His wives are buried in their own smaller pyramids nearby. Other members of his family, as well as officials, were buried in the same complex. **Archaeologists** have also found wooden boats buried nearby, which may have been to help Khufu sail through the afterlife. The pyramids show us how important the idea of an afterlife was to Egyptians!

CONTINUING THE PROJECT

Khufu's son, Khafre, continued the pyramid complex when he died. Khafre's pyramid was built around 2520 BCE, and it was about 471 feet (143 m) high. It is the middle pyramid, near the Great Sphinx. Menkaure's pyramid is the smallest of the three, at around 218 feet (66 m) high.

These pyramids weren't alone in the complex at Giza. Over time, temples, chapels, walls, and other tombs were built there. Khafre also ordered the construction of the Great Sphinx. This statue has a human head with the body of a lion. It took about 110 years to build all three of the pyramids of Giza!

The pyramid complex is a necropolis, or a large, ancient cemetery.

WOW!

Made of limestone, the Sphinx is 240 feet (73 m) long and 66 feet (20 m) high. It is one of the largest sculptures on Earth!

WHO BUILT THE PYRAMIDS?

Building the pyramids took a lot of teamwork and human strength. The Great Pyramid alone is made up of about 2.3 million limestone blocks! These had to be transported from **quarries** to the pyramid complex. Then the workers had to figure out how to get them up to their level of the pyramid. Many people think they used ramps, ropes, and sleds to move the blocks up the pyramids.

Around 30,000 people may have helped build the pyramids of Giza. The builders lived nearby in a temporary city as they worked on the pyramids. While people used to think enslaved people built them, some evidence—or clues—show that the workers were paid. Some left their marks on the pyramids through hieroglyphics.

WOW!

Each limestone block weighed about 2.5 tons (2.3 mt)!

Ancient Egyptians relied greatly on the Nile River. Could the builders of the pyramids have used an ancient branch of it?

Location, Location, Location

Why were the pyramids built in the desert? Wouldn't it be hard for people to transport things through the hot, dry desert to build them? There was a reason for this location. The Giza plateau offered high ground, which kept the pyramids safe from Nile floods. Also, some scientists now believe that a branch of the Nile River may have flowed near the pyramids thousands of years ago. This would have helped the workers transport materials and make their temporary community.

A GENIUS DESIGN

The design of the Great Pyramid is so perfect that some people think humans couldn't have created it. Some people even think aliens helped! However, humans did design the pyramids. They used their creativity and ingenuity to tackle major construction challenges. They also arranged the pyramid complex in a very thoughtful way.

One amazing feature of the Great Pyramid is that its four sides face north, south, east, and west. However, the Egyptians didn't have compasses. They weren't invented yet! Ancient Egyptians must have also had a deep understanding of math and geometry to plan the **dimensions** of the Great Pyramid.

The pyramids' designs are evidence that ancient Egyptians knew a lot about STEM—science, technology, engineering, and mathematics.

PYRAMIDS IN RUIN

Today, the pyramids look different from when they were first built. The limestone exterior was originally white. Today, the pyramids are a sandy color. The limestone was taken off the building to build the nearby city of Cairo, which is the capital of Egypt today. Erosion has worn away at the exterior as well.

Over time, tomb robbers took many of the riches that were inside the pyramids. Gold, jewels, artifacts, and furniture were stolen and sold. The bodies of the pharaohs were also taken. In fact, by the time archaeologists found Khufu's chamber, it was already empty.

While the pyramids of Giza look different today, they're still a wonder to visit.

LEARNING FROM THE PYRAMIDS

The pyramids of Giza amazed people in ancient times. As more people started exploring Egypt, they began studying the pyramids. French general and statesman Napoleon Bonaparte brought scientists and **scholars** to study the pyramids in 1798 for the first time.

Over two hundred years, explorers and archaeologists unearthed parts of the complex that had been covered in sand, such as the base of the Sphinx and several mastabas. They explored the chambers of the pyramids, finding ancient **graffiti** and artifacts. People **excavated** many parts of the site, learning more about the ancient Egyptians as they worked.

We learn more about the Giza pyramids as time goes on!

VISITING THE PYRAMIDS

Today, people visit the Egyptian pyramids to see their massive size and perfect design up close. Many visitors to the pyramids stay in the nearby city of Giza. Then, they take a car or tour bus to the pyramids.

Visitors can buy tickets to go inside the pyramids. You can take the passageway through the Great Pyramid to the King's Chamber to view Khufu's sarcophagus. Every night, there's a light show and presentation on the pyramids and Sphinx. There are some serious rules to keep visitors and the site safe, though. For example, no one is allowed to climb the pyramids!

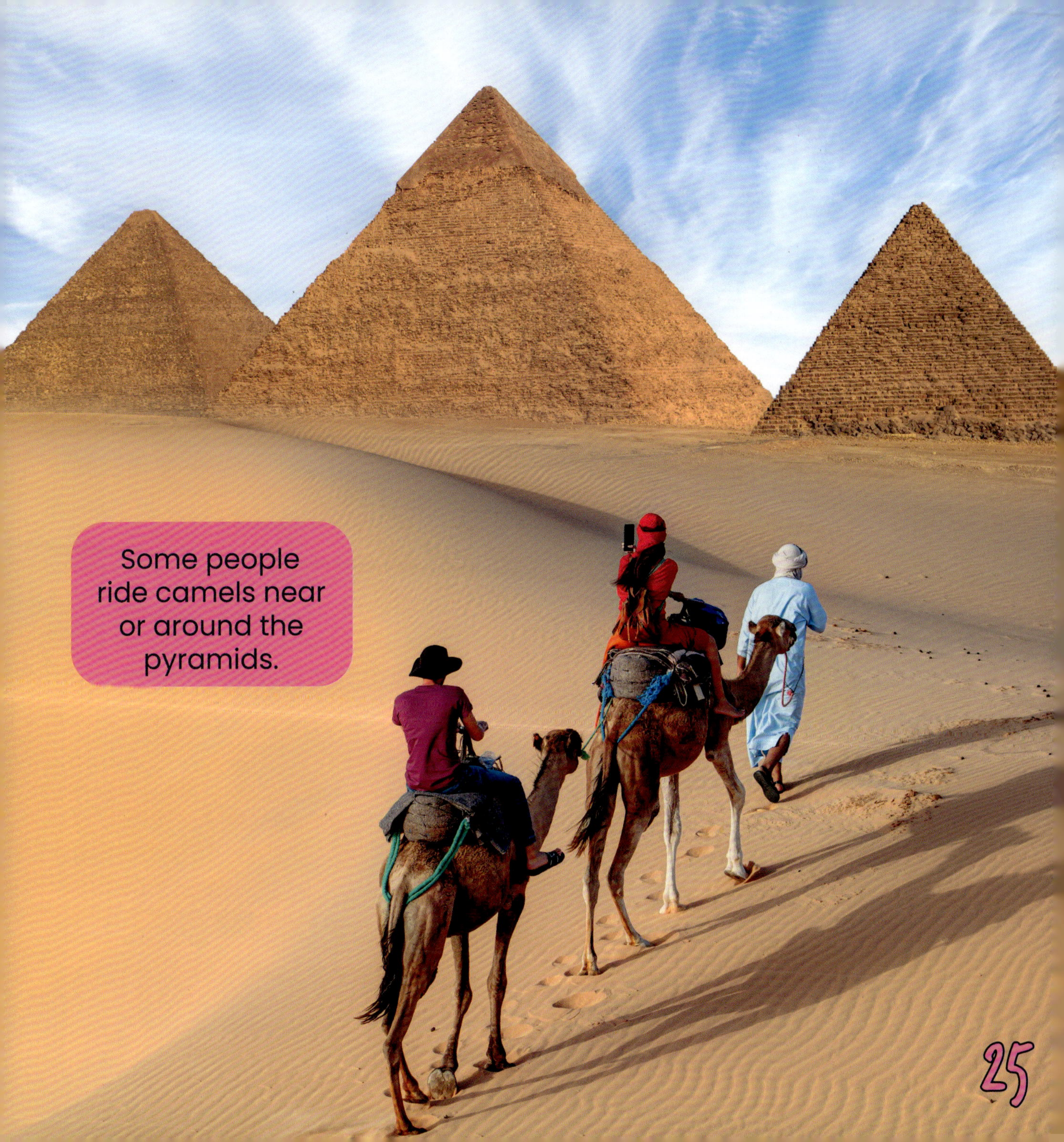

Some people ride camels near or around the pyramids.

A LASTING LEGACY

The Pyramids of Giza took over a hundred years, and hundreds of thousands of workers. Communities across Egypt may have sent workers and materials to build the pyramids. It was a huge national project, meant to show the world the great wealth of Egypt and the power of the pharaohs.

The **legacy** of ancient Egypt lives on in its amazing structures, including the pyramids at Giza. In 1979, the complex became a World Heritage Site. That means it is important to the history of Egypt and the larger world. It must be protected so it can bring wonder to people for many years to come!

WOW!

The World Heritage Site that includes the pyramids is called "Memphis and its Necropolis," and it includes the pyramid fields from Giza to Dahshur, Egypt.

YOU CAN DESIGN IT!

Imagine you have to design a pyramid fit for a king. It should be big enough to fit several chambers for different purposes, as well as anything they want to take to the afterlife. Plan out the different passageways you might use to get to each chamber and what you might construct to keep people out.

Ask yourself:
- Where will I put my pyramid?
- What materials will I use?
- How big will it be?
- How can I make it stand for centuries?

Sketch out some plans for your pyramid on a separate sheet of paper.

Bonus: Share your ideas with friends, or build a model out of plastic bricks.

You can build many different structures with interlocking plastic bricks like these.

GLOSSARY

archaeologist: A scientist who studies past human life and activities.
artifact: Something made by humans in the past.
civilization: Organized society with written records and laws.
dimension: The measure of something in one direction.
erosion: The wearing away of earth by wind or water.
excavate: To dig and remove earth in order to find something.
graffiti: Writing or drawing on a public surface, often created without permission.
heir: A person who will receive another person's property or rights after their death.
legacy: Something that is passed down from someone.
ornate: Filled with decoration and detail.
plateau: An area of high, flat land.
quarry: A place where large amounts of rock or stone are taken out of the ground.
sarcophagus: A stone coffin.
scholar: A person who attends or teaches at a school and often specializes in a field.

FOR MORE INFORMATION

BOOKS

Bradshaw, Eleanor. *20 Things You Didn't Know About the Great Pyramid.* Buffalo, NY: The Rosen Publishing Group, 2025.

Finan, Catherine C. *Ancient Egypt.* Minneapolis, MN: Bearport Publishing Company, 2022.

Jopp, Kelsey. *Giza Pyramids.* Lake Elmo, MN: Focus Readers, 2023.

WEBSITES

Ancient Egypt
kids.nationalgeographic.com/history/article/ancient-egypt
Learn more about ancient Egypt with National Geographic Kids.

Pyramids of Egypt Virtual Tour
www.youtube.com/watch?v=mOuvAJRknXk&list=PL-hr3xIvMIMU0-LruLdGBmOGDANm0H-IA&index=8
Take a tour of the pyramids with an interactive 360-degree view!

Pyramids of Giza
kids.britannica.com/students/article/Pyramids-of-Giza/630625
Read more about the Pyramids of Giza with Britannica Kids.

INDEX